DELHI, OLD AND NEW

For my aunt Saroj
and in the memory of my late uncle Ashok Setalvad

for their love, generosity, joie-de-vivre, and appreciation of beauty
in the smallest of things

Delhi, Old and New

Inkline Drawings

Kavita Iyengar

BLOOMSBURY
NEW DELHI • LONDON • OXFORD • NEW YORK • SYDNEY

First Published, 2013

BLOOMSBURY PUBLISHING INDIA PVT. LTD.
London New Delhi New York Sydney Oxford

ISBN: 978-93-82951-25-4
10 9 8 7 6 5 4 3

Published by Bloomsbury Publishing India Pvt. Ltd.
Second Floor, Building No. 4, DDA Complex, Pocket C - 6 & 7
Vasant Kunj, New Delhi 110 070

Designed and typeset by Quotes Design Studio
105, Shivam House, Karampura Commercial Complex, New Delhi 110 015

Printed and bound in India by Gopsons Papers Ltd

Disclaimer: These drawings are a selection of places and ideas that represent various facets of Delhi. Omissions should not be construed as lack of importance. Further, the drawings are not all literal, exact, nor drawn to scale. Artistic license has been used in many instances, sometimes to bring together images of objects that are not in the same place; and at other times, imagination to depict the feel of the area. The observer is therefore advised not to look for all the elements in the drawings at the physical locations described.

PREFACE

Delhi is a city with a distinctive mélange of architecture, from old living temples to the magnificent forts and European-style buildings. From mythological references in the Mahabharata to early historic citations, Delhi has been an important centre which has also linked routes across the country, but there is little that has architecturally survived from ancient times.

When the Delhi Sultanate was established at Mehrauli, the city developed its distinct Indo-Islamic style of architecture. Later, Moghul architecture blended Persian, Turkish, and Indian styles with grand, decorative, symmetric features incorporated into buildings surrounded by elaborately laid out gardens with canals and fountains. Within and around the imposing forts of Lal Kot, Siri, Tughlaqabad, and Shahjahanabad, that have withstood pillage and neglect, one finds splendid buildings. The city built by Shah Jahan within the Red Fort is still thriving and home to a large section of the city's dwellers.

The British arrived in the 1800s and occupied Civil Lines. New Delhi was built after the 1911 Delhi Durbar at which King George V and Queen Mary were proclaimed as Emperor and Empress of India. The capital was shifted from Calcutta to Delhi. Lutyens designed the new imperial capital city. Wide avenues were constructed and care was taken to line them with indigenous trees that still spread their branches majestically.

After independence in 1947, government housing colonies were built and private residential areas came up between them. Delhi has subsequently grown in all directions and the National Capital Region now encompasses contiguous urban areas in the neighbouring states of Haryana, Uttarakhand, Uttar Pradesh and Rajasthan. High-rise buildings and sprawling western-style malls, offices, and cineplexes have come up in these areas, bringing to the city a completely new skyline and horizon.

The drawings within the pages of this book are an attempt to capture the monumental glory of Delhi and provide a story of the city through its historical architecture.

The Dynasties that Ruled Delhi

Tomars-Chauhans: 736-1192

Mamluks: 1206–90

Khiljis:1290–1320

Tughlaqs: 1320–1413

Sayyeds: 1414–50

Lodhis: 1451–1526

Mughals: 1526–1857

The British: 1857–1947

Independent India: 1947 onward

TABLE OF CONTENTS

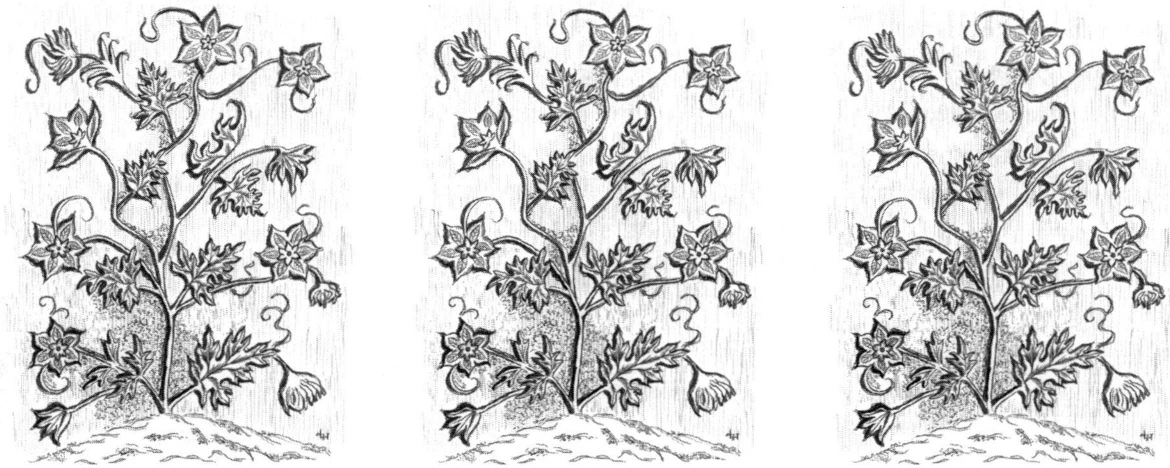

Dilli ke na the kuche,

auraq-e-mussavir the,

jo shakl nazar aayi,

tasveer nazar aayi.

The lanes of Delhi were not mere lanes, they were paintings from a painter's album, every face seen there, was a picture in itself.

Mir Taqi Mir, 1723-1810, Urdu poet

INDRAPRASTHA

Kalkaji Temple

The earliest reference to a capital city in the present location of Delhi is in legendary Indian epic *Mahabharata*, which dates to the 8th century BC. The five Pandava brothers built their capital at Indraprastha which is thought to be near the location of the Old Fort. A village called Indraprastha did exist close to the area until the beginning of the 19th century and before the British began the construction of New Delhi.

It is also believed that the Pandavas and Kauravas came to worship at Kalkaji Mandir, Delhi's oldest temple, dedicated to Kalka Ma (Goddess Kali or Durga) and the idol in the temple is said to be about 3000 years old. However, the temple was rebuilt several times and only a small portion of the structure built in the year 1734 can be seen on the top most point of the hill.

The streets were all wide and laid out excellently; and there was no fear in them of accident. And decked with innumerable mansions, the city became like unto Amaravati and came to be called Indraprastha (like unto Indra's city).

The Mahabharata

Ashoka Rock Edict

The oldest relic unearthed in Delhi, in the area currently called Okhla, dates to Emperor Ashoka (273-236 BC) of the Maurya dynasty. The rock-edict in Prakrit, written in the Brahmi script, was discovered in 1966. Through these edicts, Ashoka appealed to his subjects, irrespective of status and position, to live a pious life of *dhamma* (righteousness) in order to attain enlightenment. The location of the edict bears evidence to Delhi being a major settlement.

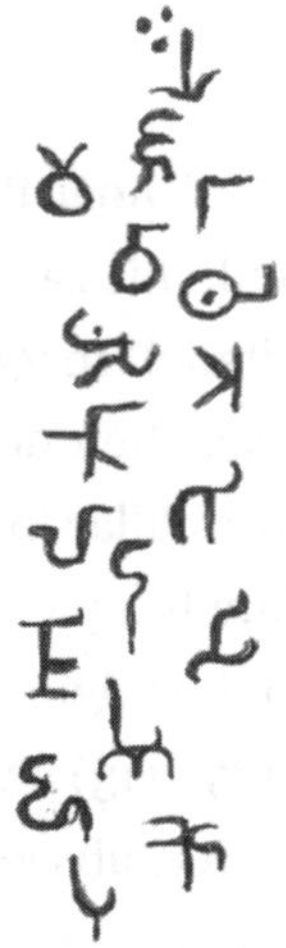

The gods who are unmingled with the people inhabiting Jambudvipa during the ages down to the present time, have now been made by me mingled with them. This is indeed the result of my exertion in the cause of *Dhamma*.

Translation of a section of the edict

DHILI, 736–1192

Qila Rai Pithora

The Tomar Rajput ruler, Anangpal I was the first ruler to build his capital in the area when he constructed Lal Kot (Red Citadel) in 736, in the current Mehrauli area. The Tomars trace their descent to the Pandavas. Anangpal II installed the Iron Pillar in its current location at the centre of the Hindu-Jain temple complex within Lal Kot. The pillar itself is dated to the reign of Gupta dynasty's Chandragupta Vikramaditya (375–413) and its weak (dhili) foundation, which allowed for its subsequent relocation, was how the city is supposed to have got its name. Anangpal is believed to have given the throne to his grandson Prithviraj Chauhan of Ajmer in 1180 and Lal Kot was renamed Qila Rai Pithora after him. Prithviraj extended the fort and built several new gates.

The carved columns of the temples are seen on the pillars of the Quwwat-ul-Islam Masjid, the first mosque in India, which was built at the site of the temples.

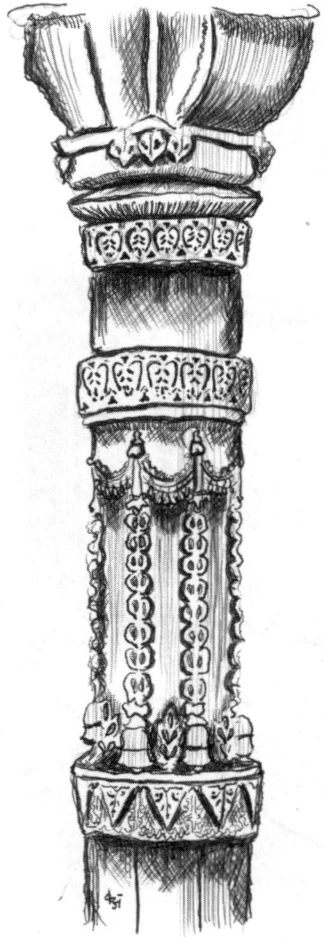

At the entrance of his [Anang Pal's] Palace, he had placed two lions, sculptured in stone. He fixed a bell by the side of the two lions, in order that those who sought justice might strike it, upon which the Rai would listen to their complaints and render justice.

Amir Khusro, 1253-1325, Musician, scholar, poet

Surajkund

Surajkund (Lake of the Sun) is an ancient reservoir near the 8th century Anangpur Dam in Haryana. Surajkund is said to have been built by the Tomar king Suraj Pal, the son of Anangpal II and a sun worshipper, in the 10th century.

At Surajkund, since 1981, a crafts mela (fair) is organized by Haryana Tourism each year to promote artisans and handicrafts from all over India.

Neeche dharti upar Ram. Beech mein lade Dhapu Dham.
Below is Earth, above is Lord Rám. Between the two, fights Dhapu Dham.

Saying in Rohilkhand on the fierce disposition of Tomar Prince Dhapu Dham who conquered territories beyond Delhi

MEHRAULI, 1206-90

Qutub Minar

Lal Kot was captured by Mohammed Ghori from the Chauhans. He left it to his slave Qutb-ud-din Aibak, who established the Delhi Sultanate under the Mamluk dynasty. Aibak built a new capital city over the debris of Lal Kot. He began construction of the Qutub Minar, the world's tallest brick minaret, in 1193 but only built the base and first storey. His son-in-law and successor Iltutmish built three more storeys. The Slave dynasty ruled till 1290 and Razia Sultan, Iltutmish's daughter, was the first woman emperor of India. The fifth and final storey of the Qutub Minar was constructed by Firoz Shah Tughlaq in 1386.

The Minar is notable for being one of the earliest and most prominent examples of Indo-Islamic architecture.

My place was *Quwat-ul-Islam* (a title of Delhi) a *qibla* (direction) of the kings of seven climes (the world). That place is Delhi, which is a twin sister of the holy paradise and true copy of *arsh* (throne of God or highest heaven) on the page of the earth.

Amir Khusro

Hauz-i-Shamsi

Hauz-i-Shamsi is a tank in Mehrauli built by Iltutmish. The Jahaz Mahal (ship palace), situated along the tank, was built much later in the Lodhi period. It is so named because it appears to be floating on the lake. The palace has intricately carved pavilions with blue tiles. The festival of Phulwalon ki sair (journey of the flower people), which started in 1720, was celebrated in the Jahaz Mahal.

In the remains of the buildings surrounding the tomb of Balban (1200-1287) in Mehrauli, we see the first arch and dome in India. It is a solid structure though it does not have the ornamentation created in the buildings built by his master Iltutmish.

Ik roz apni rooh se poocha'
"Ke Dilli kya hai?"
Tau yun jawab main keh gai,
"Yeh duniya mano jism hai
aur Dilli uski jaan."

I asked my soul
"What is Delhi?"
She replied
"The world is the body
and Delhi its life!"

Mirza Ghalib, 1797-1869, Urdu and Persian Poet

SIRI, 1290-1320

Siri Fort

The Khilji dynasty followed the Slave dynasty and Alauddin Khilji was the most prominent of its rulers. He built Siri, resembling Turkish forts of the era, in 1303 to protect the Delhi Sultanate against the Mongols. Now in ruins, the destruction of the fort is attributed to local rulers. Only few structures still stand, one being the Tohfe Wali Masjid, of which only the dome and sloping walls remain.

The Mohammed Wali Masjid, said to belong to the Lodhi era, in the Siri complex, and still has richly patterned recesses and eaves.

Alau-d-Dīn who struck his stamp upon the golden coin
Subdued a world beneath the palm of his gold-scattering hand.
By the revolution of the sky, that stamp became changed, but that gold
Remained the same in appearance, and you may see it now passing from hand to hand.

Al Badaoni, 1540-1615, Indo-Persian historian, quoting court poets

Hauz Khas

Hauz Khas (royal tank) was built by Khilji to supply water to the inhabitants of Siri. The tank was desilted during the reign of Firoz Shah Tughlaq and several buildings including a mosque, a madrasa (institution for Islamic learning), and tombs were built overlooking the water tank.

Hauz Khas village came up around the reservoir, where scholars and students of the madrasa lived. The urban village now has art galleries, boutiques, shops, and restaurants, in converted old homes along narrow alleys.

This is a reservoir ... so large that an arrow cannot be shot from one side to the other. It is filled by the rain in the rainy season, and the people in Delhi obtain water from it all the year round.

Timur, 1336-1405, Turkic ruler

TUGHLAQABAD, 1321–1325

Tughlaqabad Fort

The Khilji dynasty was followed by the Tughlaq dynasty. Its founder, Ghiyasuddin Tughlaq, built the magnificent fort of Tughlaqabad in 1321 as his capital. According to legends, it was cursed by the saint Nizamuddin Auliya because Ghiyasuddin diverted the entire city's labour towards the construction of the fort thus not allowing the saint to complete work at the bouli (stepwell) in the village. Ghiyasuddin died soon after and the citadel was abandoned due to lack of water. There were eleven rulers from the Tughlaq dynasty but only the first three generations constructed noteworthy architecture.

The tomb of Zafar Khan, the powerful Indian general of Alauddin Khilji who secured his empire by defeating Mongol invasions, is situated opposite the main entrance, within the fortress.

It (the city of Delhi) has a fine cemetery in which graves have domes over them, and those that do not have a dome, have an arch, for sure. In the cemetery they sow flowers such as tuberose, jasmine, wild rose, and flowers blossom there in all seasons.

Ibn Battuta, c. 1304-1368, Moroccan explorer

Nizamuddin Dargah

Nizamuddin Dargah, the mausoleum of one of the world's most famous Sufi saints, Hazrat Nizamuddin Auliya (1238-1325), is visited by both Muslims and Hindus. The tomb of Amir Khusro (1253-1325), his disciple, the noted scholar and musician and the royal poet of the Delhi Sultanate also lies here. The saint worshipped at the red sandstone Jamat Khana Masjid to the west of the tomb. Shah Jahan later built the pavilion around the tombs with marble arches and jalis (lattice screens).

The complex also has the tomb of Jahanara Begum (1614-1681), the daughter of Shah Jahan and his favorite wife Mumtaz Mahal (for whom the Taj Mahal was built). Jahanara played an important role in the politics of the imperial family. She supported her father who was overthrown by her brother Aurangzeb and tended to him during his years in exile at Agra Fort till he died.

Har qaum raast raahay, deen-e wa qibla gaahay,
Mun qibla raast kardam, bar samt kajkulaahay.

Every sect has a faith, a direction to which they turn,
I have turned my face towards the crooked cap.
(of Nizamudin Aulia)

Amir Khusro

JAHANPANAH, 1325–1351

Begumpur Mosque

Mohammed bin Tughlaq, Ghiyasuddin's descendent, went on to capture much of India. He built the city of Jahanpanah (refuge of the world) in 1326-27. It largely comprised a walled enclosure between Qila Rai Pithora and Siri. Little has survived and this is attributed to Mohammed bin's eccentricity in shifting the capital to Daulatabad in the Deccan and his return to Delhi later. The Begumpuri mosque, in the current Hauz Khas area, was located at the heart of Jahanpanah and served as its administrative centre, as well as a madrasa.

Muhammad bin is known for issuing a large variety of coins of various denominations. He introduced token currency in India, modeled after the Chinese. Brass and copper tokens were backed by silver and gold kept in the treasury. However, rampant forgery led to heavy losses for the kingdom.

Sultan Muhammad bin Tughluq is of all men the fondest of making gifts and of shedding blood...[known for] his generosity and courage and of his cruelty and violence towards criminals... he is of all men the most humble and the readiest to show equity and justice.

Ibn Battuta

Hazaar Sutan Palace

A building, on a raised platform in Bijay Mandal, appears to have been a place where Mohammed bin Tughlaq rested and viewed the scenic beauty around. It is believed that the ruins of the Hazaar Sutan (thousand pillar) Palace in Jahanpanah lies close to this structure.

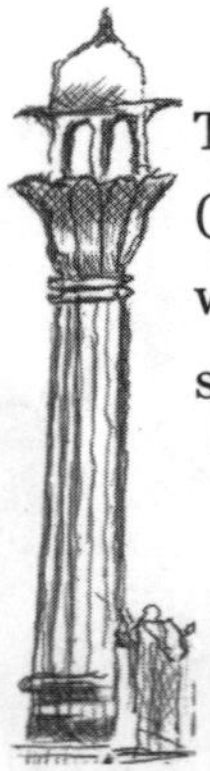

The square tomb of Sheikh Alauddin (1541–42), with its richly decorated walls and ceilings, is one of the few surviving structures in Jahanpanah.

The space between the pavilions is carpeted with silk cloths, on which the Sultan's horse treads...small catapults set up on elephants throwing dinars and dirhams among the people, and they would be scrambling to pick them up, from the moment he entered the city until he reached the palace.

Ibn Battuta

FIROZABAD, 1351–1388

Jami Masjid

Firoz Shah Tughlaq (1351-1388), decedent of Mohammed bin Tughlaq, built Kotla Firoz Shah next to the river Yamuna. It was a large enclosure of high walls, containing palaces, pillared halls, mosques, a pigeon tower and a water tank. Firoz Shah also repaired old buildings such as Sultan Ghori's tomb, the Qutub Minar, Suraj Kund and Hauz Khas. The Jami Masjid is one of the oldest and largest mosques still in use. After his death, the Sultanate became politically unstable. The Turk ruler of Samarkand, Timur, invaded India in 1398. He was so impressed by the mosque that he rebuilt a replica in Iran.

Djinns are said to be found in the ruins of Firoz Shah Kotla. According to Islam, Allah made djinns out of smokeless fire before he made humans out of clay. Every Thursday, hundreds of people gather to pray and write letters to the djinns in the hope that their wishes come true.

"Could you show me a djinn?" I asked.
"Certainly," replied the Sufi, "But you would run away."

William Dalrymple, b. 1965, Historian and writer

Ashoka Pillar and Bouli

Firoz Shah transported the Ashokan pillar (273-236 BC) from Topra, near Ambala. He built a magnificent three storeyed polished stone base for the pillar and renamed it Minar-e-Zarin (golden minar). Ruins of a circular bouli are also seen in its vicinity.

The Khirki Masjid (mosque of windows) in Jahanpanah is the only covered mosque in North India and its façade is like a fort. It was built by Khan-i-Jahan Maqbul Tilangani, the Prime Minister of Feroz Shah Tughlaq. The arched windows with perforated stone screens give the mosque its name.

These are the ways to sin, viz. fierceness, cruelty, anger, pride, envy. Let me be not ruined by these.

Ashoka, Delhi-Topra Pillar Edict III

SAYYED AND LODHI ERA MONUMENTS, 1414-1526

Kotla Mubarakpur

Khizr Khan, deputed by Timur as the governor of Punjab, took over Delhi in 1414 and established the Sayyed dynasty. It had four successors till 1451. Kotla Mubarakpur is named after Khizr Khan's son Muizuddin Mubarak Shah whose tomb is a prominent structure in the medieval village near Nizamuddin. Mubarak Shah also built a city called Mubarakabad along the Yamuna but it was destroyed. The tomb is a fusion of Tughlaq-style dome over an octagonal Lodhi-style base.

Darya Khan was a Chief Justice in the Lodhi era. His tomb in Kotla Mubarakpur is in an open pavilion style on a circular platform.

Come and cast one look upon their dust, and take warning.
For the dust is the resting-place of trusted emperors.

Al-Badaoni, upon Mubarak Shah's death

Lodhi Gardens

Like the Sayyeds, the Lodhi dynasty (1451–1526) was more concerned with restoring stability and the tombs erected in their honour, now in the Lodhi Gardens, are the few monuments from the era. The surrounding villages were relocated in 1936 to create the 90 acre park during the British Raj, which was landscaped by Lady Willingdon, wife of Governor-General of India. Sheesh Gumbad (glass dome), built during the reign of Sikandar Lodhi, used glazed tiles in its construction.

The carved columns of the Bada Gumbad (big dome) are a gateway to the attached three domed mosque and watertank.

The draught of sovereignty and glory is so sweet
That for its sake kings will shed the blood of their brethren;
Shed not the blood of the afflicted in heart for the sake of kingdom
For they will pour the selfsame draught into the cup for thee.

Al-Badaoni during Ibrahim Lodhi's reign

Jamali Kamali Mosque and Tomb

Shaikh Fazlu'llah, a renowned sufi saint during the Lodhi dynasty was known by the pseudonym Jamali (beauty). Kamali, whose antecedents are not known, was associated with Jamali and they are buried adjacent to each other in the Mehrauli area. The mosque and the tomb building were constructed in 1528-1529 but Jamali was buried in the tomb after his death in 1535.

The flat ceiling of tomb of Jamali-Kamali is painted in red and blue with Koranic inscriptions and the walls are adorned with coloured inlaid tiles inscribed with Jamali's poems. The tomb has been described 'a jewel box'.

On the day of separation from you in helplessness and loneliness nothing consoles us
but the sorrow we feel for you
O Jamali resort for protection to the door of the friend,
for our refuge is the door of the beloved.

Verse by Jamali

Agrasen ki Baoli

Agarsen ki Baoli (Agrasen's stepwell) is a small stone structure with five levels, in the heart of the city. Stepwells were a resting spot for travelers. There are no historical records as to when the baoli was built. One story is that it was constructed by a king called Agrasen who ruled over Agra before Sikander Lodhi, who built it as he was a frequent traveler to Delhi. Another version says the name was derived from Ugar Sain, the father of Kamsa and the uncle of Lord Krishna, and was built during the *Mahabharata* era.

There has been a tradition of rearing pigeons in Delhi since medieval times and they are found all over Delhi, particularly in and around monuments. The blue rock dove or feral pigeon is the wild ancestor of domestic pigeons the world over.

In this they have attained a very high degree of art so that our people (the Muslims), when they see them, wonder at them and are unable to describe them, much less to construct anything like them.

Al Beruni, 973-1048, Persian scholar

SHERGAH AND THE BEGINNING OF THE MUGHAL ERA, 1583-1545

Purana Qila

In 1526, Zahirud-din Muhammad Babur defeated the last of the Delhi Sultans Ibrahim Shah Lodi at the First Battle of Panipat and established the Mughal dynasty. His son, Humayun built his capital within the fort of Dinpanah. Sher Shah Suri, the Pashtun noble, wrested Delhi from Humayun and began building Purana Qila (old fort) over Dinpanah. Shergah served as Sher Shah's capital from 1538–1545. He introduced ornate elements in the fort's architecture. Delhi was recaptured by Humayun in 1555 and he completed parts of the unfinished fort.

The chhatris (umbrella pavilions) in the fort are reminiscent of Rajasthani architecture.

Although one's image be shown in the mirror,
It remains always apart from one's self.
It is wonderful to see one's self in another form:
This marvel will be the work of God.

Humayun, 1508-1556, in a message to Sher Shah Suri

Humayun's Tomb

Upon his sudden death in an accident in 1556, Humayun's young wife Hamida Banu Begum, built a magnificent tomb surrounded by meticulously laid gardens. This is considered the first exemplary model of Mughal architecture, second only to the Taj Mahal, which was built much later. Their son Akbar (1542-1605), considered the greatest ruler of the Mughal empire, succeeded the throne while in the midst of a war against Sikandar Shah Suri. He then moved the capital to Agra.

Carved recesses adorn the several monuments around Humayun's tomb.

At the top, on the right, are Hamīda-bānū and the child; on the left, the news is announced with sound of castanets and tambourines. In the middle, the hour of birth is being communicated to the astrologers...[and] is welcomed by music and dancing... and the Emperor was left alone, with his own people.

Gulbadan Begum, 1523-1603, Humayun's sister and biographer, following Akbar's birth

SHAHJAHANABAD AND VICINITY, 1638-1857

Lal Qila

The Mughal empire covered most of northern and central India by the end of Akbar's reign in 1605, and culture and art reached its zenith. Akbar's son Jahangir (1605-27) continued to rule the empire from Agra. His son Shah Jahan, built Lal Qila (Red Fort) when he moved the capital back from Agra to Delhi. The construction began in 1638 and took 10 years. The river Yamuna, alongside the fort, fed the surrounding moats. Delhi served as the capital of the Mughals until 1857, when Mughal emperor Bahadur Shah Zafar was exiled by the British India government.

At the entrance to the fort is Meena Bazaar, the first covered market in India. Shah Jahan was taken by the West Asian idea of a covered bazaar and thought it very suitable for the Delhi heat. The bazaar specialized in highly exclusive items such as jewelry and brocade which was not even available at the adjoining Chandani Chowk bazaar.

[Delhi] became a great imperial city...the largest and most renowned city, not only in India, but all of the East from Constantinople to Canton...Its court brilliant, its mosques and colleges numerous, and its literary and artistic fame as high as its political renown.

Percival Spear, 1901-1982, English historian

Diwan-e-khas

The emperor met special guests and dignitaries at the Diwan-e-khas (hall of private audience) while the masses were received at the Diwan-e-aam (hall of public audience). The famous Peacock throne was at the centre of the platform in the gilded hall. The throne was taken away in 1739 by Nadir Shah of Persia when he invaded the Mughals during the reign of Mohammed Shah. Later, in 1760, during the Maratha attack, the hall was looted of its silver ceiling.

The red stone walls and ceilings all over the fort are magnificently carved.

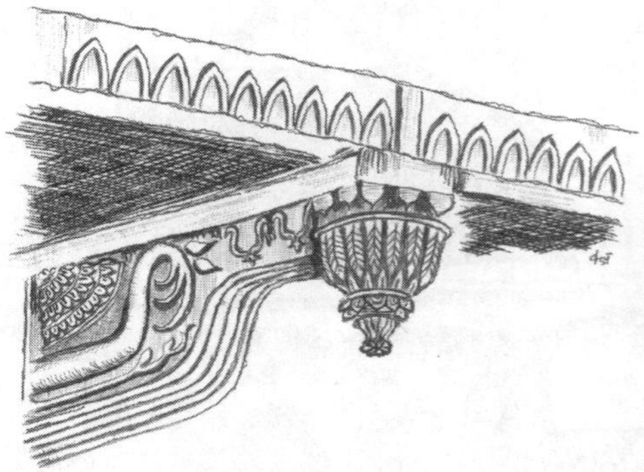

Agar fardos ba rue zamin ast
Hamin ast a hamin ast a hamin ast.

If paradise be on the face of the earth, it is this, even this, it is this.

Inscription on the Diwan-e-Khas

Jama Masjid

Jama Masjid was commissioned by Shah Jahan and completed in 1628. It is the largest mosque in India. The courtyard of the mosque can hold up to twenty-five thousand worshippers.

The details along the pillars exemplify the grandeur of the Mughal empire.

Sar zameen Dilli ki masjood-e-dil-e-gham didah hai
Zarre zarre mein lahoo aslaaf ka khawabidah hai
Paak iss ujhre gulistan ki na ho kyunkar zameen?
Khanqah-e-azmat-e-Islam hai ye sarzameen.

The region of Delhi is adored by my grieved heart
In every speck of it the ancestors' blood is asleep.
Why should not the land of this desolate garden be holy?
This region is the shrine of the grandeur of Islam.

Allama Iqbal, 1877-1938, Philosopher and poet

Chandani Chowk

Jahanara designed the grand bazaar of Chandani Chowk (moonlit plaza) within Shajahanabad. Mughal imperial processions passed through it. It still retains its historical air though it is one of the most congested parts of the city.

Royalty carried paan (betel leaf) boxes containing the accompanying condiments and it became an elaborate cultural tradition. The paan maker keeps varieties of araca nuts and paan fillings such as gulkand (preserve made of rose petals), aniseed, nutmeg, saffron, musk and kimam (tobacco paste).

Chandani Chowk symbolized solid prosperity but also the cosmopolitan spirit. It was much loved by the inhabitants, because it symbolized continuity...Continuity could be seen in the fragrance of the fresh flowers and the watered earth of the back lanes, in the five variations of Urdu spoken in the city.

Narayani Gupta, Historian

Moti Masjid

Shah Jahan's son Aurangzeb built Moti Masjid (pearl mosque) within the Red Fort in 1659 for private worship. It is a small, exquisite three domed structure in carved white marble. The Mughal Empire reached its maximum territorial strength during the time of Aurangzeb and following his death in 1707, a gradual decline of the empire began, though the dynasty continued for a further 150 years.

Pillars in the mosque, as in the pavilions, halls and baths of Red Fort, have intricate inlay work using semi-precious stones like topaz, agate, jade, jasper, malacite and onyx.

No Muslim I
But an idolater
I bow before the image of my Love
And worship her

No Brahman I
My sacred thread
I cast away, for round my neck I wear
Her plaited hair instead.

Zeb-un-Nissa, 1637-1702, Sufi poet and daughter of Aurangzeb

Jantar Mantar

Jantar Mantar (originally 'Yantra Mantra' or 'Instruments and Formulae') is an observatory for astronomy built by Maharaja Jai Singh II of Jaipur in 1724 during the reign of Mughal Emperor Muhammed Shah. The purpose was to compile astronomical tables, and to predict the times and movements of the sun, moon and planets.

The Samrat Yantra (Supreme Instrument) served as a sophisticated sun dial with graduations indicating hours, minutes, and seconds, and also a precision tool for measuring coordinates of various planets.

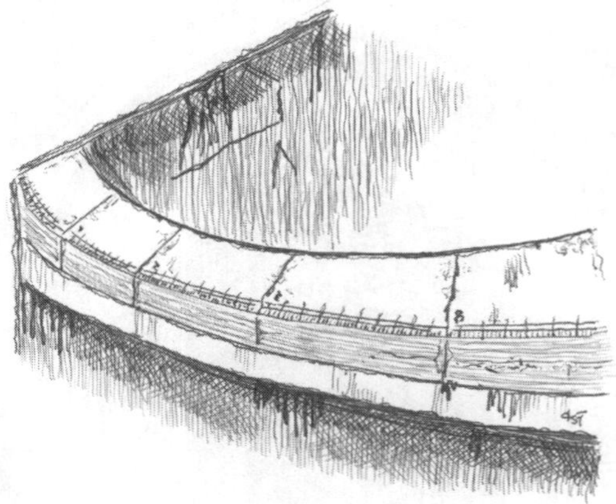

... what this observatory has is unique. There are two round buildings constructed in the form of circles and equipped with windows, in the midst of which is set a cylinder itself divided... into the hours of the prime mover (the sun).

Joseph Tieffenthaler, 1710-1785, Jesuit missionary and geographer

Gurudwara Bangla Sahib

Gurudwara Bangla Sahib is the most prominent Sikh temple in Delhi. It was originally a mansion belonging to Raja Jai Singh where the eighth Sikh Guru, Guru Har Krishan lived during his stay in Delhi in 1664. Upon the death of the Guru, Raja Jai Singh constructed a pond over the waters of the well which the Guru used to help the ailing. Later, a small temple was built by the Sikh General Sardar Bhagel Singh in 1783, during the reign of Mughal Emperor Shah Alam II.

The Sikh holy book, the Guru Granth Sahib, is placed under a colorful canopy, on a decorated seat over a raised platform, and is covered with a richly embroidered cloth. It is opened each day at random and a hymn is read as the 'hukamnama' (the order of the day).

Sri Har Krishan dhiaiyai, jis dithay sabh dukh jae.
Pray to Sri Har Krishan, seeing whom all suffering vanishes.

Sikh prayer

Havelis of Old Delhi

Havelis (enclosed place) are palatial residences or mansions which came up during the Mughal era. Opulent, combing the Hindu-Islamic architecture of the times, they typically have a central courtyard with spacious rooms around. Many were destroyed during the 1857 mutiny. Joint families who have inherited, and live in, the few surviving ones find upkeep and maintenance difficult. One of the famous havelis that attract tourists is the Haveli of Zeenat Mahal, the wife of Bahadur Shan Zafar, the last Emperor of the Mughal Empire.

Mirza Ghalib (1797-1869), the renowned Urdu and Persian poet, lived in the Hakimon ki haveli (wise persons' haveli). A very small part of the haveli, comprising half the central courtyard and a few empty rooms, is now a museum.

Ballimaraan ke mahalle ki wo pecheeda daleelon ki si wo galiyan
Saamne taal ke nukkad pe batero keq aseede...
Isee be-noorandheri see galiqaasim se
Ekt arteeb charaghon ki shuru hoti hai, ek quran-e-sukhan ka safa khulta hai
Asadullah Khan 'Ghalib' ka patha milta hai.

The lanes of Ballimaran so much like the confusing arguments
With partridge stories at the lane's corner...
In one such dull, dark street Qasim
Where a row of lit lamps starts, and a new page of poetry begins
There, the whereabouts of Asadullah Khan Ghalib are found.

Tribute to Ghalib by Gulzar, b. 1929, Poet and film director

Kashmiri Gate

Kashmiri Gate, at the northern end of the Red Fort, was fortified by the British in 1835 and later made into a double gateway, making it the only gate in the kingdom with an entrance and exit, a feature not seen in Indo-Islamic architecture. The gate gained strategic importance during the 1857 Mutiny when cannon balls were used by the British to recapture the city. 1857 marks the end of the rule of the British East India Company and was followed by direct rule of the British in India.

The Telegraph Memorial at Kashmiri Gate was erected in 1902 by members of the Telegraph Department to commemorate the loyalty of the Delhi Telegraph office staff of 1857 who stayed on duty and telegraphed news of the mutiny to Ambala in Punjab.

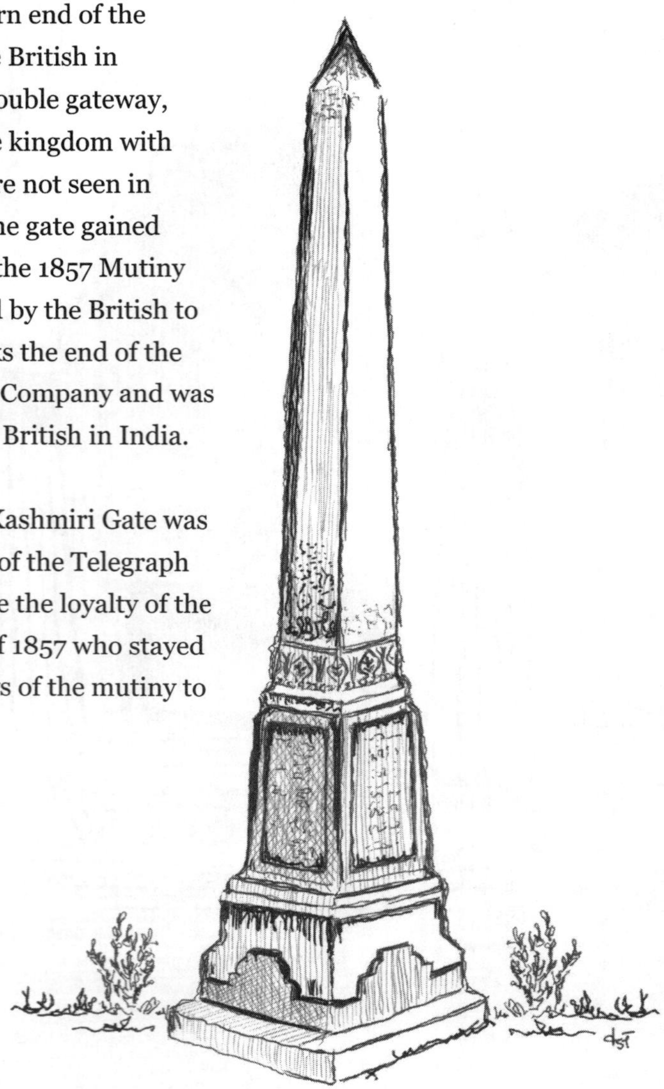

Bhai kya poochte ho? Kya likhoon? Dilli ki hasti munassar kai hangamon per thi. Qila, Chandani Chowk, her roz majma Jama Masjid ka, her hafte sair Jamna ke pul ki, her saal mela phoolwaalon ka. Ye paanchon baatein ab nahin, phir kaho Dehli kahan? Haan koi shehr is naam ka Hindustan mein kabhi tha.

What do you ask? What should I write ? Five things kept Delhi alive. The fort, Chandani Chowk, the daily crowds at the Jama Masjid, the weekly walk to the Yamuna Bridge, and the yearly fair of the flower-sellers. None of these survives, so how could Delhi survive? Yes there used to be a city of this name in the land of Hindustan.

Mirza Ghalib

CIVIL LINES AND THE BRITISH ERA, 1857-1911

William Fraser Bungalow

The British initially came to Delhi in 1803 and Sir William Fraser was assigned as the Deputy Resident Commissioner. Civil Lines was the residential areas originally built by the British Raj for its senior officers. It was the hub of European-style hotels in the city until New Delhi came into being. The William Fraser Bungalow was built in 1803. It has a unique blend of Victorian, Islamic and Indian architectural styles. It has now been converted to the office of the Chief Engineer for the Northern Railways for Construction Works.

Exquisite chandeliers in traditional styles with candle sockets hang in several old bungalows and havelis of Delhi.

Delhi is written a thousand different ways by the English, none of which is the correct one. The best in English would be Dellee and in French Delli.

Victor Jacquemont, 1801-1832, French botanist and traveller

Saint James Church

Saint James Church is an Anglican church in Delhi, built in 1836 by Colonel James Skinner, and is one of the oldest churches in the city. The basic design of Renaissance Revival style church is on a cruciform plan (Greek Cross), with three porticoed porches, elaborate stained glass windows and a central octagonal dome, similar to that of the Florence Cathedral.

The church has the graves of several prominent British officers and their families, including William Fraser and the Skinners.

Now the white road to Delhi is mat for his feet.
The sal and the *kikar* (wayside trees) must guard him from heat.
His home is the camp, and waste, and the crowd
He is seeking the Way as *bairagi* (wandering holy man) avowed!

Rudyard Kipling, 1865-1936, India-born English writer

Mutiny Memorial

The Mutiny Memorial was built in memory of British soldiers of the Delhi Field Force killed during 1857 Sepoy Mutiny, now known as the First War of Independence. It was built by the British in 1863. The architecture is Gothic and the octagonal tapering tower has an ornate façade made of red sandstone.

The memorial was renamed Ajitgarh on the 25th anniversary of India's freedom in 1972 and was rededicated to the Indians who rose up against the British in the same mutiny.

Delhi was a glorious prize, for the city was full of jewels and gold,
Besides a hundred pieces of cannon, be it told;
But dearly was the victory gained,
But in the book of fame the British are famed;
Oh, it was a glorious and heroic victory,
And will be handed down to posterity.

William Topaz McGonagall, 1825-1922, Scottish poet

LUTYEN'S DELHI, 1911-1947

The Viceroy's House: Rashtrapati Bhavan

New Delhi was built after the 1911 Delhi Durbar at which King George V and Queen Mary were proclaimed as Emperor and Empress of India. It was planned that the residence for the Viceroy and Governor-General of India would take four years to construct but due to World War I, it actually took 19 years. Its first occupant was Lord Irwin in 1931. Now, known as the Rashtrapati Bhavan (Presidential Palace), it is the official residence of the President of India. It is located on Raisina hill. With four floors and 360 rooms over a floor area of 200,000 square feet, it is the largest residence of any Head of the State in the world.

The extraordinary lace latticed wrought iron grille gates to the Rashtrapati Bhavan are a work of art by itself.

The Indo-British association may be the outer expression of the ultimate synthesis between the East and the West. If the British Empire becomes transformed into a political system based on voluntary association...it can only be on a basis of goodwill and equality.

Sarvepalli Radhakrishnan, 1888-1975, the second President of India

All India War Memorial: India Gate

The All India War Memorial, now India Gate, was built in 1931 to commemorate the soldiers of the Indian Army who lost their lives in the First World War. A statue of King George V stood under the now-vacant canopy.

The Tomb of the Unknown Soldier was constructed under the Gate in 1971. The Amar Jawan Jyoti (flame of the immortal soldier) has four burning torches which are always kept alit.

For great gallantry on the night of the 23rd-24th November (1914), near Festubert, France, when the regiment was engaged in retaking and clearing the enemy out of our trenches, and although wounded...in the face of severe fire from bombs and rifles at close range.

Citation for award to an Indian soldier in The London Gazette

Parliament House: Sansad Bhavan

The Parliament House is a distinct shaped oval building with a diameter of 560 feet whose verandah contains 144 columns. The foundation stone was laid in 1921 by the Prince Arthur, Duke of Connaught, third son of Queen Victoria, and its construction took six years. The building is made with pale and red Dholpur sandstone as is the Secretariat Building. It is spread over nearly six acres.

The Constitution of India came into effect on 26 January 1950. The Parliament Museum displays the original calligraphic copy of the Constitution.

Democracy is not merely a form of Government. It is primarily a mode of associated living, of conjoint communicated experience. It is essentially an attitude of respect and reverence towards our fellow men.

B. R. Ambedkar, 1891-1956, Chief architect of the Indian Constitution

Central Secretariat

Central Secretariat houses the most important ministries of Government of India's Cabinet Secretariat. The Secretariat buildings are two blocks of symmetrical buildings - North and South Blocks - flanking the Rashtrapati Bhavan. The building incorporates Mughal and Rajasthani architectural styles and motifs which are seen in the screens and domes.

Two sandstone columns stand in front of each bloc, representing the dominions of the British empire namely Canada, Australia, South Africa and New Zealand. On each is mounted a bronze ship sailing east.

Those who are possessed of ministerial qualifications shall, in accordance with their individual capacity, be appointed as superintendents of government departments... Without dissension and without any concern among themselves, they shall carry on their work as ordered.

Kautilya, c. 370-293 BC, Political philosopher and author of Arthashastra (Economics)

Connaught Place: Indira Chowk and Rajeev Chowk

Connaught Place, now Indira and Rajeev Chowk, is the commercial hub of Delhi. Named after the Duke of Connaught, its construction began in 1929 and was completed in 1933. The area has two concentric circles, creating Inner Circle, Middle Circle, and the Outer Circle with seven radial roads, around a circular central park.

All across the city, and especially in commercial areas, tea vendors serve chai (spiced milk tea). It is typically made in aluminum kettles and served in glasses.

Connaught Circus in Imperial Delhi represents both the high point and the end of individualistic reinterpretation of the Coliseum as a motif in town planning on a grand scale.

Andreas Volwahsen, German scholar and architect

Residence of the Commander-in-Chief: Teen Murti Bhavan

Teen Murti Bhavan was designed by British architect Robert Tor Russell and built in 1930 as the residence of the Commander-in-Chief of British Indian Army. It is so called because of the three statues at the traffic circle in front of the building. It became the residence of the first Prime Minister of India Jawaharlal Nehru who lived there for 16 years till his death in 1964.

The building, now part of the Nehru Memorial Museum, provides a glimpse of the Prime Minister's living quarters and study.

The garden [at Teen Murti Bhavan] was full of pets – little tiger cubs, a tiny panda and all manner of animals were cared for by the boys. There were a number of dogs. Sanjay's favourite pet was a crocodile, which was finally sent to the zoo, after it almost bit off Indira's fingers.

Pupul Jayakar, 1915-1997, Indian culture expert

Birla House: Gandhi Smriti

The 12 bedroom Birla House was built by the industrialist Ghanshyam Das Birla on Albuquerque Road in 1928. Mahatma Gandhi lived there for the last 144 days of his life. It is now known as Gandhi Smirti and the road is renamed Tees Janvari Marg or 30 January Road to commemorate the date in 1948 that Gandhiji was assassinated. Gandhiji held daily prayer congregations at the rear lawns in the evenings and a column is erected at the spot where he died.

The premises includes a museum which ends at Gandhiji's room and is reminiscent of his simple and stark lifestyle. It has been preserved as he left it.

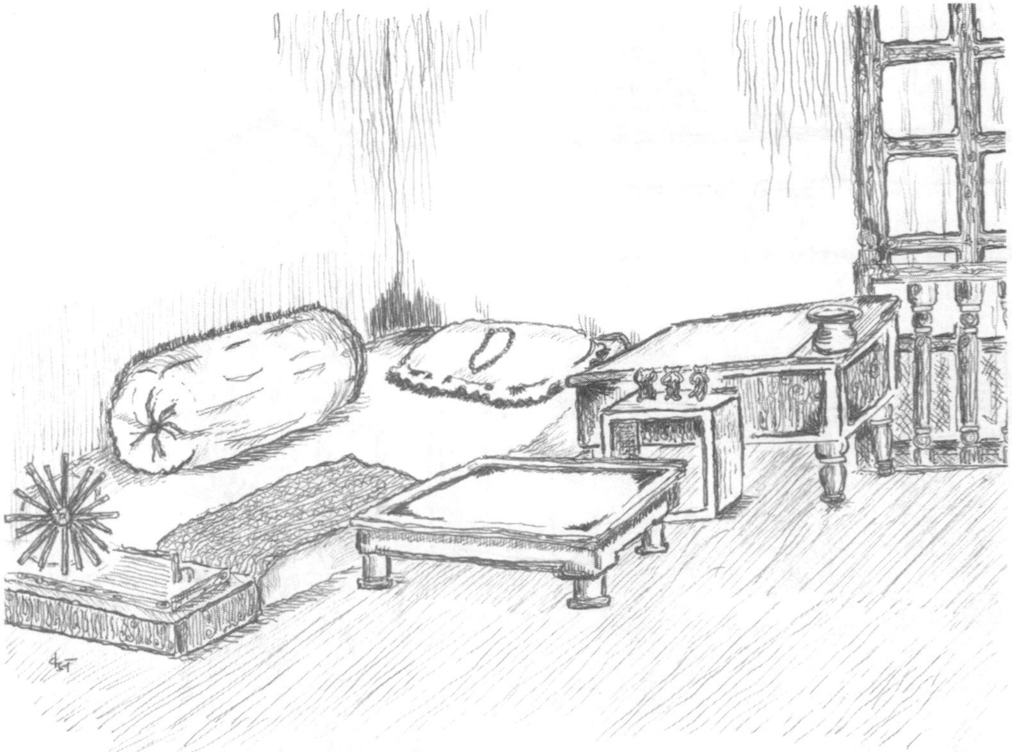

One of the last and most moving sections of Lelyveld's book has Gandhi in early 1947 walking barefoot from village to village—forty-seven in all—in the Muslim-majority area of Noakhali with his followers, now a small band, singing the Tagore song 'ekla chalo'.

If they do not answer your call, walk alone, walk alone.

Anita Desai, v. 1937, Indian novelist

हे राम
५-२० सायंकाल
३०-१-४८

Lakshminarayan Temple: Birla Mandir

The Hindu temple was built by B.R. Birla and was inaugurated by Mahatma Gandhi in 1939, with the condition that its doors would be kept open to people of all castes and faiths. The temple has many shrines but is principally dedicated to Lakshmi, the goddess of wealth, and her consort Narayana or Vishnu, the Preserver in the Hindu Trinity.

Gargoyles of fantastic beasts and gods adorn the temple complex.

Shab huii, phir anjuma-e rak'hshinda: kaa manzar khulaa,
is takalluf se, ki goyaa butkade kaa dar khulaa.

Night came, again the scene of shining stars appeared;
With such formality, as if the door of an idol-temple opened.

Mirza Ghalib

Jaipur House: National Gallery of Modern Art

Jaipur House, the residential palace of the Maharaja of Jaipur was designed by Sir Arthur Bloomfield, after the construction of Lutyen's Delhi, in 1936. The building now houses the National Gallery of Modern Art which was inaugurated in 1954. The noted German art historian Hermann Goetz was its first curator.

Sculptures are placed in the lawns and along the walkways of the building. The museum has the finest collection of contemporary art in the country.

It always surprises me to hear that those who can recognise the good in Western art are unable to do so as regards Eastern art. To me it seems incredible. But perhaps this is due to my double atavism.

Amrita Shergill, 1913-1941, Indian-Hungarian artist

A Lutyen's Bungalow: Indira Gandhi Memorial

About 800 bungalows, in what is now known as the Lutyen's Bungalow Zone, were built towards the end of the colonial era. The white, single-storey mansions have high ceilings and open verandahs that keep inner rooms away from the scorching heat of the summer. Surrounded by large gardens filled with trees and plants, they are referred to as the heart and lung of the city. They are now occupied by senior politicians, bureaucrats, and judges. One of these, the residence of Prime Minister Indira Gandhi, was converted to a museum soon after she was assassinated in 1984.

Mrs. Gandhi's favourite room in the house was her study.

Government officers were housed in low spacious flat-roofed bungalows well set back from the road, with a semi circular drive in front and a spacious area of grass and trees in the back. Whatever the size, the house and its grounds mingled beautifully and became one unit.

Sydney-Percy Lancaster, 1886-1972, British horticulturist

Modern India's Sculptures

After independence, when public areas and buildings were being planned, Prime Minister Nehru is quoted as saying that these spaces could be used to 'encourage Indian artists to function in some way'. Devi Prasad Roy Choudhary's, Gyarah Murti (eleven statues) is considered one of the greatest modern sculptures in the country. It depicts Mahatma Gandhi's Dandi March in 1931 protesting against the British empire's oppressive salt taxes.

The entrance of the Reserve Bank of India's office is flanked by a Yaksha and the Yakshini, the mythological beings who are attendants of Kubera, the Hindu God of Wealth. This combination of indigenous elements with the modern, was created by Ram Kinker Baij who is regarded as one of the foremost exponents of contemporary Indian sculpture.

Delhi has been the epitome of India's glory and disaster...Even the stones here whisper to our ears the ages of long ago and the air we breathe is full of dust and fragrance of the past, and also of the fresh and piercing winds of the present.

Jawaharlal Nehru, 1889-1964, First Prime Minister of India

Judah Hyam Synagogue

The presence of Jews in Delhi goes back many centuries, even before the British era. During the Second World War there was an influx of British and American troops and services in New Delhi for Jewish soldiers were conducted by Army chaplains. The Jewish Welfare Association was formed in 1949 and felt the necessity of a prayer hall. The main hall was constructed in 1956 and is named after Dr. Khan Bahadur Judah Hyam.

The synagogue has two Safer Torahs or hand written copies of the Torah, the holiest book within Judaism.

Yes I am, I am also a Muslim, a Christian, a Buddhist, and a Jew.

Mohandas Gandhi, 1869-1948, on being asked if he was Hindu

Pragati Maidan

Pragati Maidan (Progress Field) was built in 1982 as a trade fair and exhibition venue over 150 acres, next to the Purana Qila. It is owned and managed by Indian Trade Promotion Organisation under the government's Ministry of Commerce. There are 18 main exhibition halls along with open air theatres and food areas. The regular attractions at the venue are the India International Trade Fair, the World Book Fair, and the Auto Expo.

The National Crafts Museum is situated in a corner of PragatiMaidan. The idea and building developed over a long period of time and was completed in 1990. Run by the Ministry of Textiles, it is one of the largest crafts museums in the country with over 20,000 rare and distinctive exhibits. It is also a living, interactive museum with resident craftspersons living in the village complex which has a rural India theme.

What do you sell O ye merchants?
Richly your wares are displayed.
Turbans of crimson and silver,
Tunics of purple brocade,
Mirrors with panels of amber,
Daggers with handles of jade.

Sarojini Naidu, 1879-1949, Freedom fighter and poet, known as the 'Nightingale of India'

Lotus Temple

The construction of theBahá'í House of Worship, popularly known as the Lotus Temple, was completed in 1986. Inspired by the lotus flower, the design is composed of 27 free-standing marble 'petals' arranged in clusters of three, to form nine sides.

All Bahá'í houses of worship, including the Lotus Temple, share the nine-sided circular architectural shape, as specified by the Bahá'í scripture.

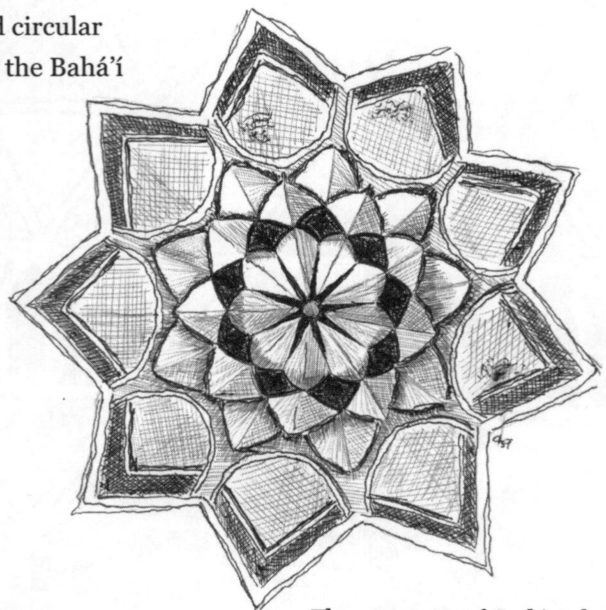

The utterance of God is a lamp: Ye are the fruits of one tree, and the leaves of one branch. Deal ye one with another with the utmost love and harmony, with friendliness and fellowship...So powerful is the light of unity that it can illuminate the whole earth.

Bahá'u'lláh, 1817-1892, Founder of the Bahá'í faith

Dilli Haat

A haat is a weekly village market but Dilli Haat is a permanent open-air crafts and food bazaar spread over six acres. Run by Delhi Tourism, it was established in 1994, and has become a venue for cultural events, including music, dance, and street theatre. A second Dilli Haat was established in 2008 at Pitampura in North Delhi.

A variety of rich and beautiful handicrafts such as embroidered silks, folk art, and furniture from all over the country, are available at the stalls.

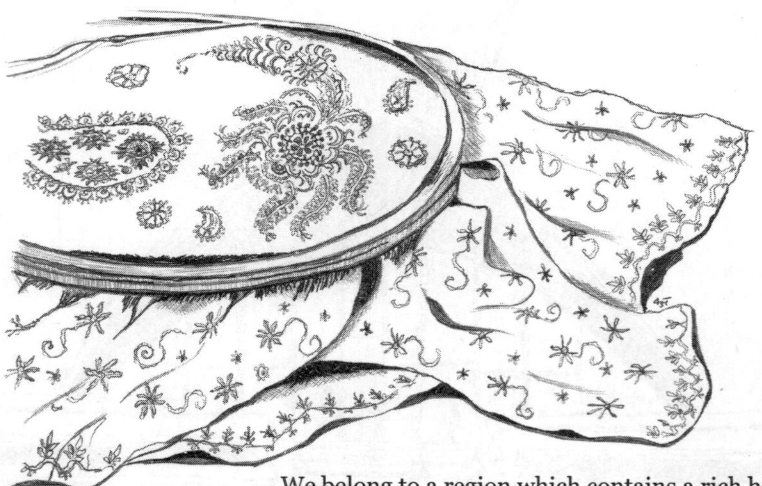

We belong to a region which contains a rich heritage of values whose significance for the present and the future cannot be minimised...beauty is not determined by the possession of expensive objects but rather by making everything we use in our daily life, no matter how mundane, beautiful...

Kamaladevi Chattopadhyay, 1903-1988, Social reformer

Akshardham Temple

The Akshardham temple is a modern landmark of Delhi along the Yamuna and is visited by about 70 per cent of Delhi's tourists. It was opened in November 2005. The central temple is made entirely of pink sandstone and Italian marble and is surrounded by landscaped gardens. 3,000 volunteers of the Swaminarayan sect and 7,000 artisans were involved in its construction.

Besides deities, the temple has ornate carvings of flora and fauna.

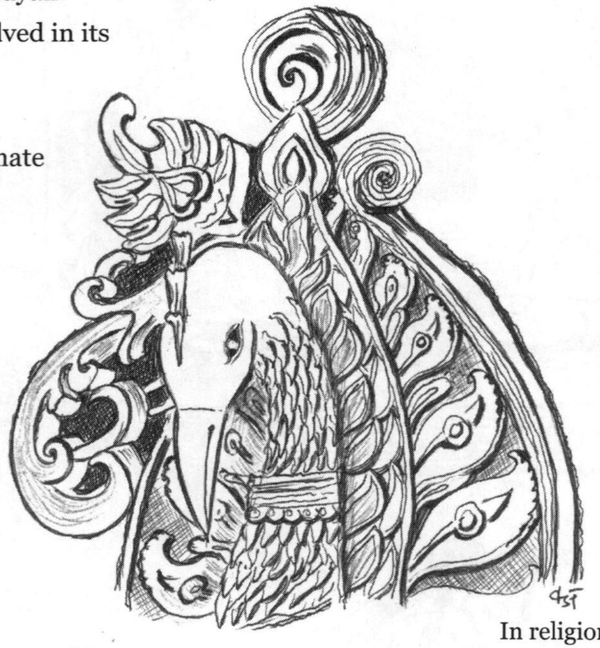

In religion, India is the only millionaire - the One land that all men desire to see, and having seen once, by even a glimpse, would not give that glimpse for all the shows of all the rest of the globe combined.

Mark Twain, 1835-1910, American author and humourist

National Capital Region

NOIDA

NOIDA (New Okhla Industrial Development Area), 20 km southeast of central Delhi, falls in the Gautam Budh Nagar district of Uttar Pradesh across the Yamuna. The Rashtriya Dalit Smarak (National Dalit Memorial) to honour Dalit icons is spread across over 33 acres and has huge statues of Mayawati, her mentor Kanshi Ram, Dr. B. R. Ambedkar, Gautam Buddha, and twenty-four large pink sandstone elephants.

Buddhist motifs have been used across the edifices in the park.

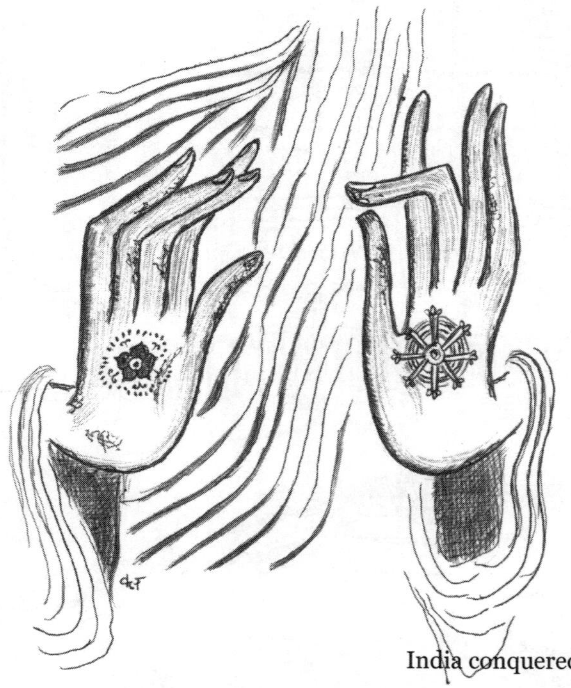

India conquered and dominated China culturally for twenty centuries without ever having to send a single soldier across her border.

Hu Shih, 1891-1962, Former Chinese Ambassador to the United States, on Buddhism

Gurgaon

Gurgaon is about 30 km south of New Delhi in Haryana. It has seen very rapid development and construction in the past two decades. A large number of multinational companies have opened their offices in the city. It has emerged as an important commercial and financial center and a major outsourcing hub of the country.

A number of galleries have come up in the city in response to the new interests of young professionals and the booming construction industry.

Making Delhineations of the Delhicate architecture...is impressed on my mind as inDelhibly as the Delhiterious quality of the water of that city.

Edward Lear, 1812-1888, English artist and poet

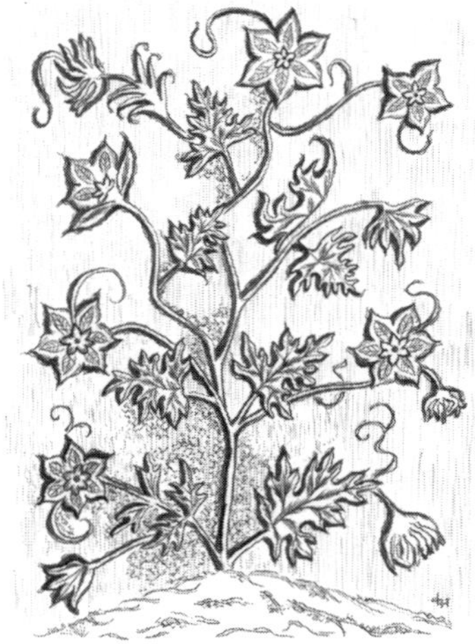 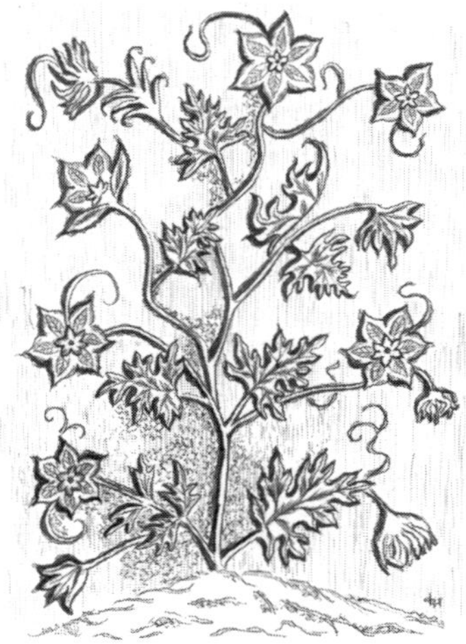 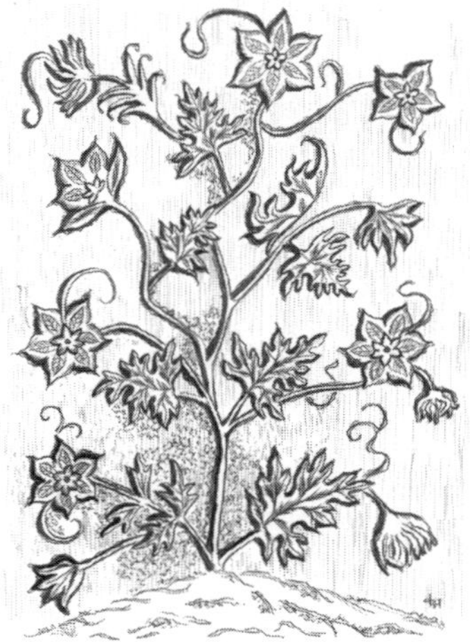

A time will come when the Indian mind will shake off the darkness that has fallen upon it, cease to think or hold opinion at second and third hand, and reassert its right to judge and enquire in perfect freedom into the meaning of its own culture and tradition.

Sri Aurobindo, 1872-1950, Indian nationalist, philosopher and yogi
The Song of Humanity, 1911

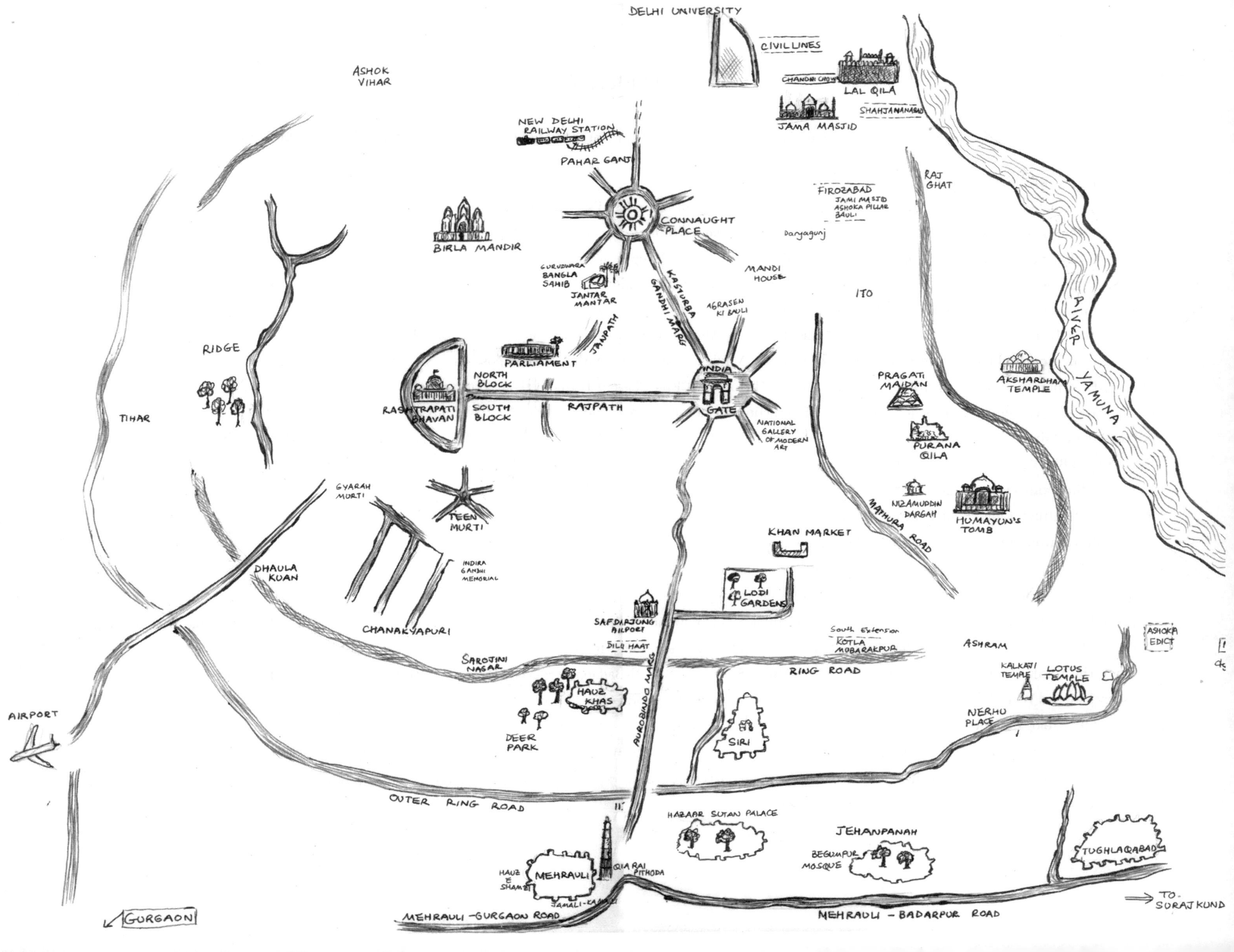
DELHI UNIVERSITY
CIVIL LINES
CHANDNI CHOWK
LAL QILA
SHAHJAHANABAD
JAMA MASJID
ASHOK VIHAR
NEW DELHI RAILWAY STATION
PAHAR GANJ
RAJ GHAT
FIROZABAD
JAMI MASJID
ASHOKA PILLAR
BAULI
CONNAUGHT PLACE
Daryaganj
BIRLA MANDIR
GURUDWARA BANGLA SAHIB
JANTAR MANTAR
MANDI HOUSE
KASTURBA GANDHI MARG
AGRASEN KI BAULI
ITO
JANPATH
RIVER YAMUNA
RIDGE
PARLIAMENT
NORTH BLOCK
SOUTH BLOCK
RASHTRAPATI BHAVAN
RAJPATH
INDIA GATE
PRAGATI MAIDAN
AKSHARDHAM TEMPLE
TIHAR
NATIONAL GALLERY OF MODERN ART
PURANA QILA
GYARAH MURTI
TEEN MURTI
NIZAMUDDIN DARGAH
HUMAYUN'S TOMB
MATHURA ROAD
KHAN MARKET
DHAULA KUAN
INDIRA GANDHI MEMORIAL
LODI GARDENS
SAFDARJUNG AIRPORT
CHANAKYAPURI
South Extension
DILLI HAAT
KOTLA MOBARAKPUR
ASHOKA EDICT
ASHRAM
SAROJINI NAGAR
RING ROAD
KALKAJI TEMPLE
LOTUS TEMPLE
HAUZ KHAS
AUROBINDO MARG
AIRPORT
DEER PARK
SIRI
NERHU PLACE
OUTER RING ROAD
HAZAAR SUTAN PALACE
JEHANPANAH
TUGHLAQABAD
BEGUMPUR MOSQUE
HAUZ E SHAMSI
MEHRAULI
QILA RAI PITHODA
JAMALI-KAMALI
TO SURAJKUND
GURGAON
MEHRAULI-GURGAON ROAD
MEHRAULI - BADARPUR ROAD

References

The compiled text is sourced from publically available information, including plaques at the site of the monuments, material from Delhi Tourism website, and Wikipedia.

Page 2, http://www.sacred-texts.com/hin/mbs/mbsi01.htm

Page 3, as translated by Vincent Arthur Smith, *The Edicts of Asoka*, Broad Campden: Essex House Press, 1909.

Page 4, as translated by Alexander Cunningham, *Archeological Survey of India Reports,* Simla, 1871.

Page 6, A.H. Bingley, *Handbook of Rajputs*, 1899, republished by the Asian Education Services 1986.

Page 8, Translation by http://www.allamaiqbal.com as cited in http://iqbalurdu.blogspot.in/2011/04/zarb-e-kaleem-115-masjid-e-quwwat-ul.html

Page 10, Amir Khusro, 18 Poems, The World's Poetry Archive, 2012, http://www.poemhunter.com/

Page 12, Al Badaoni attributes the verse jointly to Amir Khusro and Mir Hasan who were both court poets of Allaudin Khilji

Page 14, *Zafar-nama*, 'Book of Victory', Biography of Timur by Maulana Sharafu-d din Ali Yazdi composed in 1146.

Page 16, Excerpt from Ibn Battuta, *Rihla,* as cited in Indian History 2 NCERT Class 12 Textbook, Unit V https://docs.google.com/viewer?a=v&q=cache:3RxMhMY9K8sJ:dictionary.facts.co/historystudymaterial/MedievalIndia1.pdf+&hl=en&gl=in&pid=bl&srcid=ADGEEShkxwDy8SuPfalFwRdFM6KnixOxt7sV6Jb1uxnuNgEawlGFIqfRsaeWLR0JFDT9sY2Q83GLhLt_uJS9FFTID7VS1nl7-KkeQxEAzcoSwgHkBI4IYqmrSN4nR9JipnDxNeqhOW71&sig=AHIEtbRrv4sKExC78ob17ZVtlQyoTN_vRQ

Page 18, http://allpoetry.com/poem/8540995-Har_Qaum_Raast_Raahay-by-Amir_Khusro

Page 20, Ibn Battuta, *Rihla,* Book 6, http://rolfgross.dreamhosters.com/Battuta-Web/Rihla-6.htm

Page 22, Ibn Battuta, *Rihla,* Book 6, http://rolfgross.dreamhosters.com/Battuta-Web/Rihla-6.htm

Page 24, William Dalrymple, *City of Djinns: A Year in Delhi*, Flamingo, London, 1993.

Page 26, http://www.vridhamma.org/Dhamma-Messages-of-Asoka-The-Great

Page 28, The Muntakhabu-'rūkh by 'Abdu-'l-QādirIbn-i-Mulūk Shāh known as Al-Badāoni, Translated from the Original Persian and edited by George S. A. Ranking, Sir Wolseley Haig and W. H. Lowe, Calcutta, Printed at the Baptist Mission Press, 1884–1925. http://persian.packhum.org/persian/main

Page 30, The Muntakhabu-'rūkh by 'Abdu-'l-QādirIbn-i-Mulūk Shāh known as Al-Badāoni, Translated from the Original Persian and edited by George S. A. Ranking, Sir Wolseley Haigand W. H. Lowe, Calcutta, Printed at the Baptist Mission Press, 1884–1925. http://persian.packhum.org/persian/main

Page 32, http://blog.delhiheritagewalks.com/tag/jamali-kamali/

Page 34, From Preface, pages xvii and xviii of Al Beruni's India, Notes and indices by Dr Edward C Sachau, published by Kegan Paul, Trench, Trubner& Co Ltd , London 1910, http://www.columbia.edu/cu/lweb/digital/collections/cul/texts/ldpd_5949073_001/pages/ldpd_5949073_001_00000021.html?toggle=image&menu=maximize&top=&left=

Page 36, Hamida Begum quoted in *Humayun-nama: The History of Humayun* by Gulabadan Begum, translated by Annette S. Beveridge. Royal Asiatic Society, 1902.

Page 38, *Humayun-nama: The History of Humayun* by Gulabadan Begum, translated by Annette S. Beveridge. Royal Asiatic Society, 1902.

Page 40, Spear, Percival, *Twilight of the Mughals,* London, 1951.

Page 42, Quoted by Rosie Llewellyn- Jones in 'The Literary Broth', http://www.hindu.com/2001/11/04/stories/1304067e.htm

Page 44, http://iqbalurdu.blogspot.in/2011/04/bang-e-dra-093-bilad-e-islamia.html

Page 46, Narayani Gupta, *Delhi Between Two Empres 1803-1931: Society, Government, and Urban Growth,* Oxford University Press, New Delhi, 1981.

Page 47, The sweet vendor section of the painting inspired from a photo by Mark Edwards in *All India: A Catalogue of Everything Indian* edited by Reginald Massey, The Apple Press, London.

Page 48, From 'Divan-e-Makhfi' by Zeb-un-Nissa, Sufi poet and daughter of Aurangzeb, quoted in post by Raza Rumi, http://pakistaniat.com/2007/09/17/zeb-un-nissa/

Page 50, Description of Rama Yantra by Jesuit missionary Joseph Tieffenthaler, S.J who visited the observatory in Delhi in 1747, From 'Sawai Jai Singh and his Astronomy' by Virendra Nath Sharma, http://books.google.co.in/books?id=QRA2mgZnXXMC&q=jesuit#v=onepage&q=delhi%20observatory&f=false

Page 54, http://thinkloud65.wordpress.com/2011/12/27/

Page 56, http://thinkloud65.wordpress.com/2011/12/27/

Page 58, Letter from Victor Jacquemont to his father dated 8th September 1831 in "Letters from India: Describing a journey in the British Dominions of India, Tibet, Lahore and Cashmere during the years 1828, 1829, 1830, 1831" by Victor Jacquemont.
http://books.google.co.in/books?id=ibwRAAAAYAAJ&q=delhi#v=snippet&q=delhi&f=false

Page 60, Rudyard Kipling, *Song of Kabir*, http://www.poetryloverspage.com/poets/kipling/song_of_kabir.html

Page 62, http://www.poemhunter.com/best-poems/william-topaz-mcgonagall/the-downfall-of-delhi/

Page 64, 'Knowledge, Science, Culture, and the Need for Philosophy', Sarvepalli Radhakrishnan, Convocation Address, University of Mysore, 1930. Reproduced in S.K. Sharma and Usha Sharma, *Encyclopaedia of Higher Education: Convocation Addresses*, Volume 4, Mittal Publications, New Delhi, 2005.

Page 66, Citation for award of the Victoria Cross to Naik Darwan Sing Negi, 1st battalion, 39th Garhwal Rifles, one of the first recipients of the medal, From "Fourth Supplement to The London Gazette" of Friday the 4th of December 1914, http://www.london-gazette.co.uk/issues/28999/supplements/10425

Page 68, http://www.ambedkar.org/Babasaheb/quotations.htm

Page 70, Kautilya's *Arthashastra, Book II: The Duties of Government Superintendents*, Translated by R. Shamasastry, http://www.bharatadesam.com/literature/kautilya_arthashastra/arthashastra_2.php

Page 72, *Imperial Delhi* by Andreas Volwahsen http://books.google.co.in/books?id=blVQAAAAMAAJ&q=connaught+place#search_anchor

Page 74, *Indira Gandhi: A Biography* by Pupul Jayakar http://books.google.co.in/books?id=gm5JGkb2rhkC&pg=PA201&dq=indira+gandhi+teen+murti&hl=en&sa=X&ei=tc_3UP7YL8yJlQXO54DoAQ&ved=0CDMQ6AEwATgK#v=snippet&q=%20teen%20murti&f=false

Page 76, From review by Anita Desai of *Great Soul: Mahatma Gandhi and His Struggle with India* by Joseph Lelyveld http://www.nybooks.com/articles/archives/2011/apr/28/different-gandhi/?pagination=false

Page 78, http://www.speakingtree.in/spiritual-blogs/seekers/science-of-spirituality/a-muslim-poet-praises-hindu-temple&sort=new

Page 80, quoted in Amrita Sher-Gil, 'A Family Album' DVD by Navina Sundaram, 2007. http://www.iaac.us/amrita_sher-gil/cdvd.htm

Page 82, Sydney-Percy Lancaster, *A Sahib's Manual for the Mali: Everyday Gardening in India*, edited by LaeeqFutehally, 2005, Permanent Black, New Delhi. http://books.google.co.in/books?id=tmIsG6VSWt8C&pg=PA5&lpg=PA5&dq=delhi+bungalows+narayani+gupta&source=bl&ots=yNRqujc-ME&sig=Ew897hi3YD3vE7b9cUrdHeHjllk&hl=en#v=onepage&q=delhi%20bungalows%20narayani%20gupta&f=false

Page 84, Jawaharlal Nehru, 'Towards a New Equilibrium', Convocation Address, Univeristy of Delhi, 1958, Reproduced in S.K. Sharma and Usha Sharma, *Encyclopaedia of Higher Education: Convocation Addresses*, Volume 4, Mittal Publications, New Delhi, 2005.

Page 86, *A Man called Bapu*, Subhadra Sen Gupta and Neeta Gangopadhya, Pratham Books, 2008.

Page 88, http://www.poemhunter.com/poem/in-the-bazaars-of-hyderabad/

Page 90, Bahá'u'lláh, *Epistle to the Son of the Wolf* http://www.goodreads.com/author/quotes/2926126.Bah_u_ll_h

Page 92, Kamaladevi Chattopadhyay, "Of Reason Fragmented", C D Deshmukh Memorial Lecture, 1987.http://books.google.co.in/books?id=dx97VXb0JDgC&q=handicrafts#v=snippet&q=handicrafts&f=false

Page 94, http://thinkexist.com/quotation/in_religion-india_is_the_only_millionaire-the_one/170206.html

Page 96, http://thinkexist.com/quotes/hu_shih/

Page 98, http://www.muktadhara.net/page50.html

ACKNOWLEDGEMENTS

I first thank all those who have made critical contributions to this project.

My big brother Deshik Char who serendipitously appeared when I needed help most and lacked the time. He most ably and efficiently handled my difficult last-minute demands. His drawings and stories had captivated me during our childhood and I hope to work with him on future projects. My teacher Jitendra Jain who helped me find my forte in line-drawings. My art class-mates, Radhika Surana and B. Jaya Lakshmi who sat with me for hours through this till the very end, and Varsha Mathur and Ritu Bhutani who egged me onward. Sujata Kumar Suri who was most helpful beneath her no-nonsense manner. Pratap Mehta who quietly provided important inputs. Sumita Kathuria, artist, confidante, and a friend in the true all-encompassing meaning of the word, who held my hand from the beginning. Suresh Gopal, my publisher, who has been enthusiastic all the way.

There are innumerable artists whose works I have deeply admired and appreciated. Of these, two have been most inspirational for my drawings – Barbara Sansoni with her *Verandahs and Viharas* and Samir Biswas through his unmatched 'Portraits of Kolkata'. I have pored over their drawings, studied them, admired them, and envied them. I have met neither but wish to acknowledge the major role they have played in my thought process. And amongst the artists I interacted with in this context, I wish to specially thank Anand Mohan Nayak for his inputs during a wonderful afternoon spent at his home and for the time and trouble he took to look over each and every page of the sketch book. My cousin Seema Sathyu's words of encouragement have truly meant a lot to me. Krishen Khanna, in a wry manner, pointed out I was 'undoubtedly very skilled' and was incredibly generous with his time, showing me his drawings, and drawing me to think about how I would want to grow as an artist.

I also want to take this opportunity to acknowledge people from whom I have learnt valuable life-lessons.

My long-gone grandmothers, Lokamatha Iyengar and Shantha Murthy, feisty, rebellious, and creative in very different ways. My parents Vasundhara and Srinivas Iyengar, laid-back and free-thinking, who provided us the security of knowledge and books. My husband, Partha Mukhopadhyay, the completely honest critic, who pushes me to do better and never give up. My brother-in-law Sridhar, solid and dependable at all times, the rock of the family. My sister-in-law Madhavi Char, who has one of the purest, most generous hearts I have known. Deb Mukherjee, multifaced cousin and friend, for whom I did the first set of illustrations and who first suggested the idea of a book. My friend Smita Mehta, whom I can always count on. Pia Kumar, my neighbor, who pursues all her interests spiritedly. My loving cousins, nieces and nephews, especially Rashmi Gopal, Ilona Bhattacharya Roy, Neha and Niti Bagchi, Pallavi Sridhar, Shreya and Anirudh Iyengar, Yamini Char, and Sanat Nath, who expressed so much interest each time I picked up pen and paper. The welcoming Muragacha Mukherjee family and the large-hearted Bagchi clan. My parents-in-law Dipti and Kshirode Gopal Mukherjee, my sister Rekha Sridhar, my sister-in-law and brother Lakshmi and Sricharan Iyengar, and all my other family and friends, unnamed here, who have always been encouraging, and are always there for me. And the person to whom this is dedicated, my Atti, Saroj Setalvad, who, unknowing to her, has been the most powerful influence in developing my 'right side of the brain'.

salaam baalak trust

DELHI CITY WALKS
by Salaam Baalak Trust

Salaam Baalak Trust offers two walking tours in Delhi.

An exciting city walk through the streets of the inner city of Paharganj around the New Delhi Railway Station includes the living and built heritage of the area. It takes one down back streets to find ancient cultural practices which are still thriving. The walk was the brainchild of a former British volunteer, John Thompson, who trained two boys as guides and launched the program.

In 2012, the programme was expanded by developing a new heritage walk in the Old Delhi area. In this three hour walk, the emphasis is on history, architecture and life inside the walled city of Shahjahanabad. Guests walk through alleys and visit hidden places, take a rickshaw-ride to the spice market, make chai stops, climb up old buildings for rooftop views, and finally arrive at one of the largest children's homes run by Salaam Baalak Trust.

The objective of the tours is to sensitize people and uniquely engage them in the lives of children in distress. The guides are former street children who also share the journey of their own lives. Nobody knows Delhi's streets better than the youth from the Trust, who have been fully trained as guides. Thus, the walk provides them an opportunity to improve their communication and speaking skills. The proceeds go directly to the Trust, and every contribution received is acknowledged.